Maximilian Kolbe

Martyr of Charity

by
Fr James E. McCurry, OFM Conv.

*All booklets are published thanks to the
generous support of the members of the
Catholic Truth Society*

CATHOLIC TRUTH SOCIETY
PUBLISHERS TO THE HOLY SEE

Contents

Introduction 3

Childhood. 5

Franciscan 9

The Militia of Mary Immaculate 18

Return to Poland 22

Magazine Publisher 24

The City of the Immaculate 30

Mission to Japan 38

Poland Again 48

War. 52

Auschwitz 57

All rights reserved. First published 2013 by The Incorporated Catholic Truth Society, 40-46 Harleyford Road London SE11 5AY Tel: 020 7640 0042 Fax: 020 7640 0046. © 2013 The Incorporated Catholic Truth Society.

ISBN 978 1 86082 871 3

Introduction

Entering the papal vestry near the chapel of Michelangelo's *Pietà* in St Peter's Basilica, two Franciscan friars reverenced a red vestment soon to be worn by His Holiness Pope John Paul II. The two friars (one of whom is the author) would be assisting in ceremonies at which the Polish-born Pontiff would canonize his fellow countryman, the Franciscan saint Maximilian Kolbe. The scarlet colour of the chasuble was significant, betokening the Pope's decision that the new saint would be classified a "martyr."

Forty one years earlier at the Nazi concentration camp of Auschwitz, the friar-priest Maximilian Kolbe sacrificed his life to save a fellow prisoner. Hundreds of thousands of worshippers now thronging St Peter's Square would hear Pope John Paul laud the saint's sacrifice as a "martyrdom of charity." Never before had the Church elaborated a saint's dying for the faith to include the freewill laying down of one's life in love for another. Pope John Paul chose to expand the definition of martyrdom - divine love in action.

Among the worshippers in Rome celebrating that historic canonization on 10th October 1982, Franciszek Gajowniczek held a prominent place. The eighty-one year-old survivor of Auschwitz had come from his native Poland in testimony to the fact that it was he whom Fr Kolbe's self-sacrifice had spared. His old white head now ruddy under sunny skies, Mr Gajowniczek, beneficiary of charity, sat beside Mother Teresa of Calcutta, a living icon of charity. Both devotees of the new saint-martyr would receive Holy Communion from the Pope.

At the end of the canonisation Mass, the Holy Father dramatically embraced Mr Gajowniczek - two Poles sharing a common Catholic faith, which had been forged on the anvil of suffering and fortified by the heroism of their fellow Pole Maximilian. The memory of Auschwitz was foremost on the minds of everyone in Rome as the canonisation ceremonies solemnly transpired. No one four decades earlier - least of all Fr Kolbe's Nazi captors - could have envisioned this moment. In an astonishing reversal of fortune, the vilified inmate of an obscure prison camp was now being glorified among the ranks of the saints, forevermore to be honoured by billions of Catholics on altars throughout the world.

Childhood

The death of a saint gives testimony to a lifetime of cultivating virtues. In this way, the life of St Maximilian Kolbe proves instructive. His schooling in heroic charity began at home. Born in the village of Zduńska Wola, near Łódź, on 8th January 1894, the second of five sons - of whom the two youngest would die in infancy - he was baptised with the name Raymond. From earliest childhood, the future saint found himself enthralled by tales of Polish heroes, and he even fancied himself a knight engaged in chivalric battles.

Poland at that time did not exist politically as a distinct nation on the map of Europe; it was partitioned between three powerful empires, Russia, Germany and Austria-Hungary. Nonetheless, Raymond's patriotic father Juliusz Kolbe instilled a strong sense of Polish identity in his sons. He would relate stories from Polish history, and read to his sons from Polish literary classics like the epic *Pan Tadeusz* of Adam Mickiewicz, and the novel *With Fire and Sword* by Henryk Sienkiewicz. Young Raymond inherited from his father a zeal that was at once both religious and patriotic. A patriotic Pole did not recognise the Czar of Russia as his true sovereign, but rather the Queen of Heaven, to whom

Polish kings of yore had formally entrusted the governance of their realm.

For Poles like the Kolbes, religion and politics became interwoven. To be Polish was to be Catholic, faithful to "God and Fatherland." The Kolbe family would sometimes journey on pilgrimage to the national shrine of Jasna Góra. This "Bright Mountain" in the southern Polish town of Częstochowa housed the medieval sanctuary of the Black Madonna - a venerable icon bejewelled and crowned to denote the status of the Blessed Virgin Mary as the sovereign Queen of the Polish realm. The Kolbe family kept a small replica of the regal icon in their kitchen. At one key moment of his youth, Raymond Kolbe enthusiastically vowed to the Virgin Queen that he would be her liege and dedicate himself in battle for her cause. Later in life, as he pursued his religious vocation, Raymond would come to understand that God wanted his patriotic Marian vow to be transformed by the deeper spiritual light of religious consecration.

Raymond's pious and strong-willed mother, Marianna Dąbrowska Kolbe, zealously imbued her sons with a religious sensibility. She exacted from them a disciplined obedience to the simple tasks of daily life. She and her husband were hard-working weavers, labouring over home looms. They belonged to the Third Order of Saint Francis, a lay movement now called the Secular Franciscan Order. As Franciscan Tertiaries, they embodied a spirit of poverty and piety, which aimed to sanctify the ordinary moments of family existence through prayer and work. They were committed to the conversion and sanctification of peoples' hearts for the sake of building up the Church, after the example of St Francis of Assisi (d. 1226).

Having moved to the village of Pabianice, Marianna Kolbe practiced a quaint local custom. Using her skills with fabric and stitchery, she made miniature Franciscan habits for her young sons to wear at Mass in their parish church of St Matthew on Sundays and holy days. Pious habits or not, boys will still be boys. Hence, on one occasion, Mrs. Kolbe lamented that young Raymond was becoming too cheeky. With exasperation she inveighed, "Raymond, what will become of you?!" Duly chastened, the lad, about ten years of age at the time, took seriously his mother's plea of concern.

Shortly afterward, while praying alone in St Matthew's at the side altar of Our Lady of Victory, Raymond underwent a mystical experience. He saw a vision of the Blessed Virgin Mary offering him two crowns, the white crown of purity and the red crown of martyrdom. With childlike abandon, Raymond accepted both crowns, and thereupon began consciously striving to be as pure and self-sacrificing as possible. He told no one of the vision, except his mother, who had noticed a remarkable change in the boy's demeanour. Mrs Kolbe kept secret this story of her son Raymond and the two crowns until shortly before her own death in 1946. Having survived her husband and five sons, the elderly Marianna Kolbe gave testimony to officials of the Order of Friars Minor Conventual in Poland, detailing the miraculous event that had taken place in Pabianice some forty years earlier.

Inscribed over the entrance portal of St Matthew's in Pabianice are Jesus's words "*Sequere me*" ("Follow me"), from the Gospel of Matthew (*Mt* 4:19). Those words would hold prophetic significance for the teenage Raymond and his elder brother Francis when the Minister Provincial of the Franciscan Friars Conventual, Fr Peregryn Haczela, preached a parish mission at St Matthew's in 1907. The Friar's challenging message resonated so powerfully with the Kolbe family's ardent Franciscan ethos that the brothers Francis and Raymond Kolbe would soon apply for admission to the Order's formation programme, desiring to follow Christ in the footsteps of St Francis.

Franciscan

Joining the Franciscan Order in 1907 meant that the thirteen-year-old Raymond and his fifteen-year-old brother Francis would need to travel from Czarist-controlled central Poland to the Austrian sector further south. Lacking documentation, the two boys were hidden by their father under the hay of a farmer's wagon, and thus transported across the frontier towards Kraków, passing near Częstochowa en route. Later, the Franciscans of Kraków would transport the two vocation prospects to their large seminary further east in Lwów, a city which is now in southwestern Ukraine.

Eventually the third Kolbe brother, Joseph, would join his other two seminarian-brothers. With all three living sons in the Franciscan houses of formation, the parents Juliusz and Marianna made an extraordinary decision about their own future. With ecclesial permission, and taking perpetual vows of celibacy, they separated so that Juliusz could also join the Franciscans as an oblate and Marianna enter a convent of contemplative Benedictine nuns.

Despite his intentions, Juliusz did not persevere with the Friars. Ever the patriot, he moved to Częstochowa, and subsequently seems to have joined Piłsudski's Legions to fight against the Russians. Some accounts report that he was captured and executed. His death remains a mystery. Marianna Kolbe eventually transferred to the Felician Sisters of the Franciscan Third Order, and remained a domestic oblate of their community in Kraków for thirty-two years until her death. Buried in the habit of a Tertiary, she reposes in the common tomb of the Felician Sisters at the same cemetery in Kraków where the parents of Pope John Paul II are buried.

Francis Kolbe, the saint's eldest brother, did not persevere in his Franciscan vocation either. Like his father, he followed a patriotic inspiration to fight for Polish freedom. His life became troubled and problematic, however. Francis's errant ways, a fractured marriage with Irene Friebling, the abandonment of his young daughter Aniela, and his painful struggle with depression and human weakness would become a continuing source of concern for the rest of the Kolbe family over the next two decades. Francis's plight awakened in the future St Maximilian a compassionate understanding of the challenges posed to family life in modern times. Like his saintly younger brother, Francis would be killed in World War II. The two of them had one last poignant meeting less than a year before the war. Francis confessed his prodigality and his lament at having left the Order. St Maximilian commended him to the watchful care of the Immaculate Virgin, and Francis bade his brother "Go with God."

The youngest brother Joseph did indeed persevere as a Franciscan Friar Conventual. According to religious custom, both Raymond and he were given new religious names at their respective investitures in the Franciscan habit, as each commenced his novitiate year in the Order's formation programme. Raymond became "Maximilian": Joseph became "Alphonse." Friar Alphonse Kolbe would eventually profess vows and be ordained, but he died prematurely in Poland after a sudden attack of appendicitis in December 1930.

Ironically, of the Kolbe brothers, it was Friar Maximilian who suffered the poorest health; yet he outlived all of them. Having completed novitiate in Lwów, he was sent by his Franciscan superiors for philosophy and theology studies in Rome, Italy. Altogether, Friar Maximilian would spend seven years at the Order's Collegio Serafico on the Via San Teodoro, a small lane linking the ancient Roman Forum with the Circus Maximus. His seminary faced the palace of the Caesars, now in ruins atop the Palatine Hill. Originally apprehensive about life in a city that he perceived as pagan, Friar Maximilian underwent a process of profound spiritual growth in the Eternal City. Gradually between 1912 and 1919, Kolbe the Pole and Kolbe the friar would merge into Kolbe the apostle. His religious consecration would intensify, and the focus of his life's mission would sharpen.

Some of Friar Maximilian's fellow seminarians would later give testimony about their classmate. Their comments reveal details about the personality and humanity of this quiet friar-seminarian from Poland during the early years of his Roman formation. One Polish-American friar, Fr Austin Maciejewski, observed: "I was ordained in 1913 - the year that Kolbe came to Rome as a student…Young priests like myself had to go out every morning to offer Mass in the abandoned churches of Rome. I chose Kolbe to accompany me as my altar boy. I liked the boy - I took a yen to him…He was a good boy, already a saint when in college - you could see it beaming from his person - a mild, humble boy, very friendly, agreeable, and open."

Another Polish-American friar, Fr Peter Hajna, lived with Maximilian at the spartan Collegio in Rome for two years: "There was not a bathtub in the whole college; we all washed with basins and a pitcher of cold water; one toilet for the whole wing of at least thirty boys. Kolbe never complained, as the rest of us did." After the canonisation, the nonagenarian Fr Peter offered further insights into the character of the future saint: "Kolbe and all the Polish boys were very studious. Kolbe was aloof from the other fellows; he did not mix much. He had a good saintly face; a very quiet young man. A Jesuit priest used to come every Saturday for confessions. Kolbe used to wait considerately until the end of the line of penitents, because he knew he took longer than all of the rest of us. We thought he was a bit scrupulous, but

I will say this, that in the time I lived with him, I never heard an idle word nor any criticism from his mouth."

Important events at Rome

Six inter-related events indelibly impacted Friar Maximilian's Rome years: the Order's solemn consecration to the Sacred Heart of Jesus and related devotions to the Immaculate Conception of the Blessed Virgin Mary; the seventy-fifth anniversary of the conversion of Alphonse Ratisbonne in conjunction with the Miraculous Medal; the two-hundredth anniversary of modern Freemasonry marked with anti-Catholic demonstrations through the streets of Rome; the onset of tuberculosis, an affliction that would plague Friar Maximilian for the rest of his life; the founding of the *Militia Immaculatae* ("Militia of the Immaculata") movement on 16th October 1917; and Friar Maximilian's priestly ordination on 28th April 1918.

Hanging prominently in the sanctuary of the Collegio Serafico's chapel, where Friar Maximilian spent several hours praying each day, an enormous oil painting depicted the Sacred Heart of Jesus appearing to St Margaret Mary Alacoque and indicating to the visionary that St Francis of Assisi was the saint most dear to his heart. As Friar Maximilian immersed himself in the Franciscan tradition, he meditated upon the primacy of Christ and his kingdom of charity. Through this optic, the Lord's "heart" served as a symbol of universal charity. Accentuating this Franciscan thesis, a special ceremony took place in the Collegio's chapel in June 1913, consecrating the Collegio, in union with the entire Franciscan Order, to the Sacred Heart of Jesus. This event led Maximilian to a deeper theological and religious understanding that the divine plan for the purpose of life, and the reason for God's creation of the universe, was the establishment of the kingdom of the Sacred Heart of Jesus. Kolbe became passionate about the transformation of the world into a civilization of love.

In the same year as Friar Maximilian came to know the Order's consecration to the Sacred Heart, a large statue of Our Lady of Lourdes was also dedicated in the same Collegio's chapel. The halo around the Virgin's head contained words spoken in 1858 by Our Lady to St Bernadette at Lourdes: *Que soy era Immaculada Councepciou* ("I am the Immaculate Conception"). That statement, with all that it implies, became a lifelong mantra in Maximilian's prayer and theological reflection. Following the Order's historical tradition, Friar Maximilian affirmed the inseparable link between the primacy of Christ and the unique role given to humble Mary as the first beneficiary of the Redeemer's saving power. He would write: *"The Immaculata knows the secret of intimate union with the Sacred Heart."* This statue of the Immaculata, along with the Sacred Heart painting, remains in place through the present day, at the same site in Rome, now called the "Convento San Massimiliano Kolbe."

While working on his doctorate in philosophy at the Pontifical Gregorian University, and subsequently a doctorate in theology at the Pontifical Faculty of St Bonaventure, Friar Maximilian discovered a comfortable harmony between profound theological teachings and simple pious devotions. Illustrative of this harmony was his discovery of the "Miraculous Medal" as a tool for evangelisation. This "Medal of the Immaculate Conception" had its origins in Paris in 1830, and soon acquired the tag "Miraculous" because of the numerous prodigies associated with it.

In January 1917, the Collegio's rector, Fr Stephen Ignudi, was reading aloud to the seminarians a meditation commemorating the seventy-fifth anniversary of the conversion of Alphonse Ratisbonne through the instrumentality of the Miraculous Medal. Ratisbonne, a prominent Swiss banker and rabid anti-Catholic, had been challenged by a friend to wear a "Miraculous Medal" for a few days as a "harmless experiment." If nothing happened, then Ratisbonne's claim that Catholics were nothing but a lot of superstitious pietists would be confirmed. What could be the harm? The "experiment" produced the opposite effect, and Ratisbonne experienced a mystical vision of the "Woman" of the Medal, in the Church of Sant' Andrea delle Fratte near Rome's Spanish Steps. One cannot underestimate the powerful impact that this meditation had on the impressionable Friar Maximilian.

He would carry a pouch of Miraculous Medals for the rest of his life, and regard them as a sign of Mary's role as a stimulus for the conversion of hearts to God.

A month later Rome witnessed massive demonstrations against the Church and the papacy by the Freemasons. The latter were observing the two-hundredth anniversary of the founding of the Grand Lodge in London. Their aggressive antagonism towards Catholicism turned vicious and blasphemous. Freemasonry claims, without much hard evidence, to have originated in medieval labour guilds. Whatever their actual origin, masonic lodges had in many cases become secretive societies with occult overtones, deist principles, and socio-political platforms. Underlying their ideology was a philosophy of materialism and secular humanism, a fundamental denial of all things supernatural. They pilloried Catholicism, its hierarchical structure, and its sacramental values. Friar Maximilian, deeply saddened as he witnessed public expressions of hatred against the Church he loved, became convinced that only supernatural means could avail to counteract these forces.

Friar Maximilian intuited that modern times would come to be dominated by forces bent on excluding God from every sphere of public life. He began formulating a strategic plan of evangelisation that would restore a biblical understanding of the world as God's domain, the Church as God's presence in his domain, humanity as God's children, Jesus Christ as brother to the human race, and Mary Immaculate as Mother to all the exiled children of Eve. Alert to the signs of the times, Maximilian became convinced that a positive spiritual offensive would serve as the best defence against contemporary godlessness.

The Militia of Mary Immaculate

The Friar's strategic planning suffered a setback in the summer of 1917 when he was suddenly stricken with a lung haemorrhage while playing football with his confrères at the friary known as "La Vigna" across from Rome's Baths of Caracalla. The diagnosis was tuberculosis. By the grace of God he recovered, but would periodically go through lengthy periods of relapse throughout the rest of his life. Pain, excruciating headaches, shortness of breath, weakness and fatigue would be his constant companions. Undaunted and faith-filled, Friar Maximilian soldiered on. He would allow nothing would to undermine the urgent sense of mission that animated his zeal for the kingdom.

A watershed moment that would define the rest of Friar Maximilian's life took place unheralded in a small room of the Collegio on the night of 16th October 1917. Gathered with six fellow young friars (two Romanians and four Italians), Maximilian read aloud in Latin from a small sheet of paper. There he had handwritten the charter of a new movement which he had been inspired to found, the "Crusade of Mary Immaculate" (in Latin, *Militia Immaculatae*).

The group of seven friars would forge among themselves a bond of spiritual knighthood. Their purpose was the conversion of the enemies of the Church, the sanctification of the human race, and the unity of Christians. The conditions for membership were the personal act of offering oneself to the Blessed Virgin Mary as an instrument and collaborator in her work for the Church, and the wearing of the Miraculous Medal as a sign of that consecration. The means of accomplishing the Crusade's purpose would be daily recitation of the prayer on front of the Miraculous Medal and using every possible circumstance for proclaiming the Gospel, catechesis, and faith formation. The honoured title of Our Lady that the new movement would foster was the *Immaculata*, referring to the Immaculate Conception. Its biblical inspiration was the "Protoevangelium" passage from the book of Genesis (3:15), where the Lord God proclaims that the Woman and her Offspring would crush the head of the ancient serpent.

The religious superiors of Friar Maximilian recognised the authenticity of his inspiration in founding the Crusade of Mary Immaculate. Eventually they would obtain Vatican recognition of the movement as a "pious union" and a public association of the faithful. From the quiet seed of seven obscure friars, the movement would spread worldwide. It has continued to grow through the present time, inspiring and attracting Catholics of all types. Among them, on 9th December 1991, Mother Teresa of Calcutta recited the formula of "total consecration to Mary" written by Maximilian Kolbe, and enrolled herself in the Crusade.

Not all Franciscan friars follow a vocation towards priestly ordination. Within the Franciscan calling of Friar Maximilian, however, the priesthood beckoned as a further way of his identifying with the purity and sacrifice of Christ the High Priest. As a friar, his priestly ordination would be put at the service of the strategic plan for building the kingdom. All the various facets of his Roman formation converged on 28th April 1918 in the Church of Sant' Andrea della Valle, when the Cardinal Vicar of Rome, Basilio Pompilj, conferred upon Maximilian the Sacrament of Ordination to the Holy Priesthood.

One day later, the newly ordained Fr Maximilian chose to celebrate his first Mass at the altar where the Blessed Virgin had appeared to Alphonse Ratisbonne in the Church of Sant' Andrea delle Fratte. On the holy card souvenir of this Mass, the humble new priest had imprinted a Polish quotation from King David's prayer in the second Book of Samuel, *"Who am I, Lord, that you have brought me thus far?"* (2 S 7:18). He further quoted, in Polish, St Francis of Assisi's constant prayer *"My God and My All."* A third Polish quotation appears at the bottom of the holy card. Mindful of his Franciscan tradition, and the great friar-theologian of the Immaculate Conception John Duns Scotus, he printed the phrase attributed to the latter during his years at the University of Paris: "*Permit me to praise thee, O Holy Virgin; give me strength against thine enemies.*"

Fr Maximilian remained in Rome for another year to complete his doctoral studies. On his first Christmas as a priest, he offered his three traditional Masses in a church not far from the Collegio on the same Via San Teodoro, the Church of Sant' Anastasia. Indicative of the his thoughts in these early days of his priesthood is the Mass intention for which he offered the second of his Christmas Masses: "*Pro amore usque ad victimam*" *(For love even unto victimhood)*. That inscription was handwritten in Latin by Fr Maximilian in the local Mass register.

Return to Poland

By the summer of 1919, World War I had ended, and Poland had at last obtained its political independence. The zealous twenty-five-year-old Fr Maximilian returned to his homeland in July, stopping en route to offer Masses at the tombs of St Francis and St Clare in Assisi, and in the Holy House of Our Lady in Loreto. His first assignment in Poland would be at the great Franciscan church in Kraków, which had stood at the foot of Wawel Hill for nearly seven hundred years. Dominating the interior of the Franciscan basilica is the enormous 19th-century stained glass masterpiece of God the Creator by Stanisław Wyspiański, Polish artist, playwright, poet, and patriot. The modernistic window visually reinforced for Fr Kolbe the Franciscan ethos of God's almighty dominance over all creation, and humanity's humble duty to foster the divine order in modern life.

Among the duties that were assigned to Fr Maximilian at the Church in Kraków was overseeing the teenage altar servers. One of the young lads was thirteen-year-old John Chodacki, who impressed Fr Kolbe as having a potential religious vocation. John later recalled that even a future saint could lose his patience with cheeky teenagers. John and three of his mates went swimming without permission in the river Vistula during high water time. Afraid that they might drown, Fr Kolbe did not hesitate to reproach them sternly. He called John a "skunk." John did eventually decide to join the Franciscans, and was given the name Friar Jeremy.

Fr Maximilian continued to take a special interest in Jeremy's vocation as a friar. He visited Friar Jeremy at the novitiate in Lwów, and later encouraged him as a priest to develop his talents in liturgical music and classical composition. They would share jokes, dreams, fears and hopes. On one occasion, while walking together in Lwów, Father Maximilian told Jeremy that in the future people from this planet earth would travel to the moon, not by aeroplane, but by rocket ship. He shared with Jeremy his anguish about the presence of the Devil, the spread of materialism in Poland, and the threat of Communist Russia. Years later, Fr Jeremy would remember Fr Kolbe's pensive reflections about those issues, and his hope that the Franciscan Order could be a peace-giving force for good amidst a secularised world of conflict.

Magazine Publisher

Indeed Fr Kolbe had impressed his convictions upon the Chodacki lad from the earliest days of their acquaintance, when the teenager was still acting like a "skunk." Maximilian confided to Chodacki his plan to use the mass media as a tool for evangelisation. Fr Kolbe aimed to launch a magazine. His objective was simple and direct: to publicise the "Crusade of Mary Immaculate" in Poland as an antidote to the growing post-war secularism of his beloved fatherland. Eventually he obtained the required permission from his Franciscan superior, the Minister Provincial, to publish a religious journal, the *Rycerz Niepokalanej ("Knight of the Immaculata")*. The Provincial, however, told him that the Order had no money to invest in the project. Hence, Fr Kolbe would need to raise his own funds.

With neither money, nor press, nor editorial offices, Fr Kolbe remained supremely confident. He knew that the first editions of the magazine would need to be outsourced. One day he presented the altar server Chodacki with a request. He had a list of print shops in Kraków, and needed to visit them in search of the one that would offer the most economical deal for printing the *Rycerz*.

He needed Chodacki's help navigating the complicated streets of Kraków. Through the labyrinth, Fr Kolbe and the future Friar Jeremy paced. After visiting several sites, Maximilian finally settled on the second of the printers as his best prospect.

The fledgling publisher's first problem was to pay the printing bill. The issues could not be collected and circulated until that happened. He begged lay friends and strangers for money, but still was five hundred marks short. Kneeling at Our Lady's altar in the Franciscan basilica, he entrusted the desperate economic situation to her maternal intercession. Rising from prayer, he noticed on that very altar an envelope addressed "For you, O Immaculate Mother." Inside was the exact amount of five hundred marks. Writing later about this timely discovery, Fr Kolbe would pose the question: *"A Coincidence?"* Providence would make the presses roll.

In January 1922, the first five thousand copies of the *Rycerz* were published and distributed. The theme of the first editorial written by Fr Maximilian in this first edition was happiness. *"Where is Happiness?"* he asked rhetorically. After examining false or fleeting paths to happiness, the editor answered his own query: *"Only in God!"* This theme would set the moral tone and establish a positive leitmotif for his publishing apostolate over the next two decades. As the magazine gathered popular momentum, the apostolate of the press would make new demands upon Fr Maximilian, who began formulating a strategic plan for the work.

He would need to purchase his own printing press, so that he could set up shop in the Kraków friary. Divine Providence would intervene again, in the person of Fr Lawrence Cyman, a Polish-born Franciscan Friar Conventual and parish priest of St Stanislaus Church in Chicopee, Massachusetts, USA. The American visitor took a keen interest in Fr Kolbe's apostolate, and offered him an initial one hundred dollars, a large sum of money at the time, towards the purchase of his first printing press. Fr Kolbe would nickname the press "Babcia" ("Grandma"). In the ensuing years, Fr Cyman would continue to be a supportive benefactor of Fr Kolbe's media projects, as would several more American friars.

Some of Fr Maximilian's fellow friars in Kraków were less than kind, including the guardian of the Kraków friary. There was some envy, some mockery, and some resentment at what was perceived to be a disruption of the quiet and well-ordered life in the friary. Some gave him the sobriquet "Marmalade," deriding his "sweet" piety. Others criticized what they perceived to be an exaggerated Marian tone in his writings. Maximilian did not hesitate to answer genuine complaints, with quiet erudition. His two doctorates proved helpful in that regard. The irrational barbs he humbly tolerated with patience and good humour.

The community grows

By the autumn of 1922, however, it became clear that a new centre for Fr Maximilian's publishing mission would need to be found. The Franciscans had a large friary a long distance away, in the city of Grodno, situated within a Polish-controlled sector of White Russia (now the independent nation of Belarus). In October of that same year, Fr Maximilian re-located the publishing ministry to Grodno. Various friars from throughout the Province contributed articles to the magazine. Meanwhile, a steady stream of new recruits for the Order joined him in the media apostolate at Grodno. Among these friars was a young zealot named Friar Zenon Żebrowski - more commonly known as "Brother Zeno." For many years thereafter, he would become Maximilian's faithful factotum - truly a jack-of-all-trades.

Indeed, like Brother Zeno, many of the friars attracted to this new Franciscan ministry of the press were skilled and talented craftsmen. They embraced the Franciscan vocation of brotherhood as a way of husbanding their natural talents for the glory of God and the spread of his kingdom. This they did in the context of a conventual community that integrated work with prayer and mission. These friar-brothers did not follow a call to priesthood. As a friar-priest surrounded by a majority of friar-brothers, Fr Maximilian would pioneer the Order's attempts to restore the charism of Franciscan community life that had been seriously hampered in the previous century due to war and the forced political secularization of religious houses. Grodno became an important locus for the renewal of the Order's *vita communis* ("common life").

Meanwhile, during all of his Kraków and Grodno years, Fr Maximilian periodically suffered relapses of his tuberculosis. The medical treatment required lengthy periods of convalescence in sanatoriums run by religious sisters in Zakopane, southern Poland, amidst the Tatra mountains. His brother Fr Alphonse Kolbe was assigned to the Grodno community. This comforted Maximilian; nonetheless the pain of separation from his religious community weighed heavy on the heart of the ailing friar. Still young and afire with zeal, his forced confinement nonetheless gave him further time to pray, read, reflect, and plan. He learned to play chess - and saw in its strategic dynamics an image of the spiritual battles he would later fight. He also used the time as an opportunity to study the lives of saints and blesseds, particularly those who suffered debilitating illnesses like his own.

When Fr Maximilian received an unpublished manuscript about a young American friar, who had lived a saintly life and died while still a seminarian, he determined to publish it on the presses of Grodno in 1923. Entitled *A Short Life of the Deceased Seminarian Louis M Figlewski, Franciscan*, this forty-five page monograph represents

Fr Maximilian's first venture in redacting and publishing lengthier texts. Its author was the deceased seminarian's brother, Fr Alphonse Figlewski, a Polish-American member of the Franciscan Conventual Province of St Anthony in the USA. The young Friar Louis Figlewski had been the first friar of the St Anthony Province to be called by Sister Death. The fact that the cause of his death was tuberculosis did not escape the notice of the book's publisher, who suffered from the same illness.

The primary thrust of the Grodno apostolate remained its preoccupation with the ideals of the Crusade of Mary Immaculate - endeavouring to foster the moral values of the Gospel in an increasingly materialistic and secular society. Harnessing the media for the purposes of conversion and sanctification proved no mean task. In 1926 Fr Maximilian addressed the Polish Catholic Congress, assembled in Warsaw. His topic revolved around the responsibility of a journalist. He alerted his colleagues to the threats posed by the inappropriate use of the media for pornography and obscenity. Participants in the Congress discussed the need for a Catholic daily newspaper, in order to present a Christian perspective on secular news and political events. Fr Maximilian began cultivating the hope of expanding his own media ministry to include such a "daily." This would eventually be realised in 1935, when the friars began publishing *Mały Dziennik* ("Little Daily").

The City of the Immaculate

Throughout the mid-1920s, as the Crusade spread and the circulation of the *Rycerz* increased, the number of vocations to the Order in Grodno multiplied rapidly. Within five years, the facilities were proving to be too small. Larger and more sophisticated machinery was needed. Moreover, the location was too remote for effective management of the magazine's distribution. Fr Maximilian's expansive strategic plan envisioned the establishment of an enormous friary in the environs of Warsaw, the nation's capital. This would be a Franciscan centre for evangelisation, where the friars would live and work, embodying the ideals of St Francis with a renewed spirit of brotherhood - all entrusted to the maternal care of the Blessed Virgin Mary under her title, the Immaculate Conception. It would be called *Niepokalanów* - "City of the Immaculate."

With typical reliance on the providence of God, Fr Kolbe undertook to find the proper site for this City of the Immaculate. His prayers began producing results, when on the feast of the Franciscan saint, Anthony of Padua, 13th June 1927, Maximilian asked the advice of a visiting priest. The priest suggested that Maximilian make enquiry about a tract of land in the village of Teresin (Sochaczew), which seemed well suited to his purposes. Situated on a railway line about twenty-five miles northwest of Warsaw, the Teresin property was owned by a member of the local nobility, Prince Jan Drucki-Lubecki.

The Prince was an astute businessman, unmarried, in his late twenties. He and Maximilian had never met. Since the Prince also owned land in Grodno, he agreed to meet Fr Kolbe during a visit to Grodno in July. For two consecutive days, the Prince met Fr Maximilian and his brother Fr Alphonse Kolbe. Shortly thereafter, the Prince agreed to donate five hectares of land, with the stipulation that a specified number of Masses be offered at the new friary in perpetuity for the deceased of the Drucki-Lubecki family. The Kolbe brothers were delighted. The following month, Maximilian and Alphonse set up a statue of Mary Immaculate in the middle of the fields at Teresin that the Prince had offered.

Complications soon arose, however. The stipulation of perpetual Masses was too formidable a condition for Maximilian's Franciscan superiors to approve, and the Provincial rejected Prince Lubecki's offer. Maximilian and Alphonse bore the sad news to the Prince. The latter queried what would become of the statue of the Immaculate that Maximilian had prematurely installed as "proprietress" of the land. Maximilian told the Prince that the statue should remain there, since the consecration had placed the estate under her protection. Shortly thereafter, the Prince was riding past his land, noticed the statue, and immediately felt a deep warmth within himself. At that inspired moment, he knew that he must give the tract to the friars without any conditions. Within weeks, the construction of the new friary of *Niepokalanów* was fully underway. Within a decade, *Niepokalanów* would become the largest Franciscan friary in the world, numbering over seven hundred and fifty men.

Prince Lubecki's involvement with Fr Kolbe did not end with the gift of land. He became one of Maximilian's trusted advisers and confidants. The Prince was captivated by the impact that the personality of Maximilian had on people. The Prince sensed something supernatural or mystical about the person of Fr Kolbe. Though always joyful and smiling, a teller of humorous quips, Maximilian also displayed a serious side, tenaciously holding to principles. The Prince noted a sense of urgency about everything that Maximilian did, not that he ever gave the impression of hurrying. Maximilian placed great importance on doing as much as possible as soon as possible.

Occasionally the Prince and Fr Kolbe would have conflicting points of view about the proper way to conduct business - honourable men disagreeing honourably. One day, while visiting the City of the Immaculate, Prince Lubecki noticed a costly new printing press from Germany. He asked Maximilian to see his financial records and book-keeping. He replied, "We do not keep books. If we need to do this, Our Lady will provide." Aghast, the

Prince expressed consternation. On the following day, a new brother entered *Niepokalanów*; it turned out that he was an experienced accountant. The astonished Prince later remarked: "Fr Maximilian was right; I was wrong."

No topic of conversation had greater urgency for Maximilian than the subject of Our Lady. In his view, she provided the spiritual power to the motors of *Niepokolanów*, all in humble service to God and his kingdom. Prince Lubecki found himself spellbound as Maximilian shifted topics from business to spiritual matters. He probed Maximilian's teaching about the spirituality of "total consecration" to the Immaculate Virgin Mary, and the relationship of that spirituality to the apostolate of the Crusade, in which he had enrolled himself. He noticed that Maximilian would use several different Polish words in various contexts to describe the phenomenon of "consecration." For the rest of his life, the Prince (who died in 1990) kept five of those words in heart, as "facets of the diamond," or nuances that when placed together helped him to make his Marian consecration "total."

Five facets of Fr Kolbe's diamond

The five words mentioned by Maximilian to Prince Lubecki all derive from the Polish ecclesiastical tradition of consecration, which Maximilian had inherited. His Franciscan formation further refined his understanding of consecration. Accordingly all five words had a bearing upon the full and integral meaning of that "total consecration to Mary" which Fr Kolbe lived and taught. As a mnemonic device, the listing below gives the first three or four letters of each term before the word itself:

- KON - *Konsekracja* - This is an action of the Church, setting aside a person or an object for a sacred purpose. It confers "religious" status upon the one who is consecrated.

- POŚ - *Poświęcenie* - This is an action by the self, setting oneself aside for a sacred purpose. The root of the word is "*święty*" (holy, sacred). It refers primarily to the gift of oneself to God, who is holy, for his exclusive use. By analogy, it was sometimes used in reference to one's relationship with Mary.

- ŚLUB - *Ślubowanie* - This is the commitment of oneself to God by making vows. The root of the word is "*ślub*" (vow). While this term refers both to religious vows and to marriage vows, it was also used in Poland to refer to the vows made in 1656 by King Jan Casimir of Poland, committing the country to Our Lady as her "vassal".

- ZAW - *Zawierzenie* - This word means entrustment, or putting of oneself in a relationship of trust. The root of the word is "*wiara*" (faith). Underlying the act of consecration to Mary is the establishment of a relationship of trust with her.

- ODD - *Oddanie* - This word means dedication, or giving oneself back to God and Mary as an oblation. Its root is "*dać*" (to give), tending towards "*oddać się*" (to give oneself back/away). It is more anthropological than theological.

Maximilian wrote his "*Akt Oddania*", a prayer of "total consecration to Mary" which still circulates in multiple languages throughout the world, wherever the Crusade movement is active. Prince Lubecki repeated the same consecration prayer daily until his death.

Not only Prince Lubecki, but everyone who came into contact with Fr Maximilian Kolbe at *Niepokalanów* and throughout his life, testified to the formative place that Marian consecration held in his character development. The call to self-offering as a Pole and a friar marked him indelibly as a "man of consecration." A little-known character study of Fr Maximilian Kolbe, done in 1945, four years after his death, corroborates these personality traits and personal characteristics of the future saint. The study depicts him as a man whose integrity demanded that he be consecrated in the fullest sense possible.

The character study was based upon a graphological analysis of Fr Kolbe's handwriting, evidenced in a letter written at *Niepokalanów* in 1929, and provided by a Polish-American acquaintance of Maximilian, Fr George Roskwitalski OFM Conv. The Franciscan

Friars Conventual in Italy had pioneered the modern science of graphology (handwriting analysis). Adhering strictly to these scientific principles, Friar Fernando Vesprini OFM Conv., did the study of the Kolbe script without knowing the writer's identity. Fr Vesprini was an associate of the famous Fr Girolamo Morretti OFM Conv., who is considered the founder of the science. Admitting a margin of subjectivity in interpretation, the analyst presents findings overwhelmingly consistent with subsequent testimonies about the character, personality, and capabilities of the future saint as recorded by eyewitnesses in their depositions for his canonisation:

1. *"He has a rather profound intelligence, acute, and assimilative to quite high degrees. He is of fine discernment...One might marvel at the vastness of his knowledge and his keen sense of observation... present in abundance and with some originality...He applies himself doggedly and he has a very fine memory...He is able to make good choices because of his facile and assimilative understanding...He has good discernment in psychological matters. His instinct in psychology is noteworthy for its insights into cognitive and affective areas...Even though very talented and capable, he shows in addition moderation in speech, and handles himself quite well with a certain sweetness of wit and a delicate affectivity.*

2. *"In the desire of preserving his own self-identity, he seeks something to lean on. He would not be capable of true initiatives without some help. Once this is supplied, however, he marches on without looking back...He feels a strong need of finding understanding and affection. Should he entrust himself to another person he would be fully committed and dedicated... Of modest demeanour, and a bit shy, and humble, he enjoys telling stories and airing out his complaints but only in confidence and not with many words...Of a total affectivity, he comes close to being passive, almost feminine in nature...At first glance, he might even seem unpolished and incapable but with his intimates he is truly very precious...He is possessed of a heart that instinctively and with authority could grasp all the nuances of love and affectivity."*

Noteworthy conclusions can be drawn from this analysis of Fr Kolbe's character. It profiles him at the time when *Niepokalanów* had already been in operation for two years. It offers new insights into Maximilian's human need for self-surrender to a higher power, a dynamic that his mature spirituality of consecration would build on. Grace builds upon nature. Finally, it illuminates the way in which Marian spirituality forges a balance in Fr Kolbe's ministry between a nearly passive affectivity on the one hand and a tenacious determination on the other.

Mission to Japan

"Leaning on" the Immaculata, and *"marching on without looking back,"* Fr Kolbe displayed the *"tenacious determination"* described above when in 1930 he requested from his Franciscan superiors permission to establish a new mission of the Order in Asia. *Niepokalanów* was just barely on its feet, less than three years old, when its founder felt confident enough to leave it in the hands of his Franciscan confrères - totally consecrated to Our Lady - while he extended its evangelisation mission on another continent. He prepared for the mission by going on a brief trip to Rome through Germany and France in January of 1930.

While in Rome, Fr Maximilian sought permission from the Minister General of the Order to go to the Far East as a missionary. The General and he went to the Church's primary office for the missions, the *Propaganda Fidei* - the College for the Propagation of the Faith. A committee of the *Propaganda* would need to endorse the mission. They did. However, it still did not specify whether the first destination would be China, Japan, or India. One of the people whom Maximilian met at the *Propaganda* was a young Japanese seminarian, Joseph Satowaki (who would later become the Cardinal Archbishop of Nagasaki). When Maximilian told the young Satowaki that he hoped to work as a missionary in Asia, the seminarian suggested, "Why not Japan? Go to Nagasaki, where there are many Catholics!" Somewhat more intent on China, Maximilian nonetheless filed "Japan" prominently in his memory.

Returning from Rome to Poland, Fr Kolbe stopped to pray at five shrines where he invoked the patronage of the saints to whom he was closest. He entrusted his missionary impulse to their heavenly intercession: St Francis in Assisi; St Anthony in Padua; St Bernadette in Lourdes; St Catherine Labouré at the Rue du Bac in Paris; and St Thérèse the Little Flower in Lisieux. The Paris site was where the Miraculous Medal originated. Maximilian had already distributed thousands of those medals, dear to him since his days as a seminarian. He had come to call them his "bullets" in the battle to win souls. In Lisieux, he renewed his "pact" with St Thérèse - a spiritual accord that he had made with her on the day of his first Mass at Sant' Andrea delle Fratte, when he promised to work towards her cause of sainthood, asking that she take charge of his priestly missions. A quaint note about his visit to Thérèse's family home *Les Buissonnets* in Lisieux is the comfort he found catching sight of the chess set that remained among Thérèse's belongings. Thérèse, like him, understood the need for tactical plans of action.

Sailing from Marseilles in March 1930 with four friar-brothers (including Brother Zeno) as his chosen companions, Fr Kolbe and his fellow missionaries surveyed the mission landscape. Having stopped in Singapore, Vietnam, and China, Fr Kolbe finally selected Nagasaki, Japan. He had left behind two of the friars in Shanghai to negotiate with the local bishop, while he and the other two friars continued by ship to Japan. They landed there on 24th April. The following day Fr Kolbe offered public Mass in Nagasaki's Oura Cathedral, the oldest Catholic Church in Japan, site in 1865 of the memorable "Discovery of the Hidden Christians," an event still commemorated by Japanese Catholics annually on 17th March. All of the friars, including Maximilian, grew beards, the symbol of missionaries in that era.

Without money, or knowledge of the Japanese language, life would be enormously difficult for these missionaries. Their zeal and trust in Providence trumped their deprivation. The friars who lived with Maximilian in Japan later attested their conviction that he could not have endured Auschwitz had he not endured first the hardships and suffering of Nagasaki. During those years, his tuberculosis took a perilous turn for the worse. X-rays of his lungs from that period, still preserved in the friary in Nagasaki, indicate that only one quarter of one lung was functioning normally. Afflicted by constant fevers, violent headaches, shortness of breath, and extreme exhaustion, he found himself increasingly dependent upon his Franciscan confrères in order to carry out his daily duties.

Immediately after the friars' arrival in Japan, Fr Kolbe sought the blessing of the local bishop, Januarius Kyunosuke Hayasaka, and began making contacts, so that the publishing apostolate might commence. Remarkably, one month to the day after arriving in Nagasaki, Fr Kolbe sent a telegram to his Provincial in Poland, informing him that the first Japanese issue of *Seibo no Kishi* ("Knight of the Immaculata") had been published - ten thousand copies. Fr Kolbe wrote the articles in Latin, and enlisted the help of a few Japanese priests, as well as a Methodist pastor, to translate the Latin into Japanese.

The next task at hand was to establish a Japanese counterpart of *Niepokalanów* - a Japanese City of the Immaculate. Fr Maximilian searched various locales of Nagasaki, and prayed for discernment. Most of his advisers recommended that the new friary and publishing house be situated in the central section of the city, Urakami, where the majority of Catholics lived. Fr Kolbe resolutely rejected that proposal, simply indicating that the Immaculata wanted her "Garden" to be built on the outskirts of the city, in the Hongochi district on the opposite side of Mount Hikosan.

This decision would later prove to be an inspired choice - some of the brothers indeed would call it "miraculous." For, when the atomic bomb fell upon Nagasaki on 9th August 1945, the epicentre of the devastation was very close to Urakami (where the rosaries of people praying in the new Catholic cathedral can still be seen melted into clumps). Miraculously, the Franciscan friary in Hongochi escaped destruction, and would become a refugee centre. By then, of course, Fr Maximilian had long since returned to Poland and died at Auschwitz. It would be Brother Zeno who became the hero of Nagasaki at the end of the war, ministering day and night to the victims of the bomb, in the "ant villages" where they set up temporary housing for the refugees. Zeno the Franciscan is commemorated today by the Japanese people with a Memorial Tower on Mount Fuji.

A new garden for the Immaculata

The stable Franciscan presence in Nagasaki truly began on 16th May 1931, when Fr Kolbe dedicated his Japanese City of the Immaculate, giving it the name *Mugensai no Sono* - "Garden of the Immaculate". He and the friars had lived and worked in temporary rented housing near Oura for a year. Maximilian would remain at *Mugensai no Sono* through 1936. One of the first things constructed at the new friary was a Lourdes Grotto, high atop the hillside. Nearly every day, Fr Maximilian would climb the one hundred steps to the Grotto. Because of his infirmity, the brothers would sometimes need to support him on either side. On stronger days, he used a stick. The statue of Our Lady of Lourdes in the grotto was a gift from Fr George

Roskwitalski in America. It depicted the mystery of the Immaculate Conception.

Not surprisingly the writings of St Maximilian from this period in the Japanese Garden of the Immaculate exhibit a growing mystical tone about the relationship of Mary to each of the three Divine Persons of the Holy Trinity. His theological reflections in Nagasaki take on a decidedly Trinitarian focus. He begins to write about Mary Immaculate as "complement" of the Most Holy Trinity - a title that he had learned from reading texts of the Fathers of the Church. He contemplated in Nagasaki the figure of Mary Immaculate wholly imbued and infused with the love of the Father, the Son, and the Holy Spirit. He contemplated the entire love of the Trinity being poured into the humble and pure Virgin Mary.

The friars who lived with Maximilian at *Mugensai no Sono* considered him a mystic. They likened his experiences at the hillside Grotto to the mountaintop experience of Moses - sites where these holy men met God. The friars described Maximilian's face as glowing when he would descend from the Lourdes Grotto, just as the Scriptures described Moses. Brother Sergiusz suspected that it was during these mystical moments in Nagasaki that the Blessed Virgin Mary appeared to Fr Maximilian, offering him the promise of heaven. Years later, in an intimate setting at *Niepokalanów*, Maximilian confided to his closest confrères that he had been given a promise of heaven. His favourite hymn was a French song *J'irai la voir un jour* ("One Day I Shall See Her"). It evoked for him the glimpse of heaven that he had experienced the Virgin vouchsafing to him. He first learned it in Rome as a student, and often asked the friars of Grodno, *Niepokalanów*, and *Mugensai no Sono* to sing it, either in French or in Polish.

True mystics must still deal with ordinary human affairs, and keep their feet firmly planted on *terra firma*. Problems galore confronted Fr Kolbe throughout his six years in Nagasaki. Not all of the friars were unanimous in their support of his ideals. One young Polish friar-priest, Konstanty Onoszko, struggled mightily with doubts about the authenticity of Fr Kolbe's Marian piety. He suggested that it was exaggerated and theologically unsound. Maximilian patiently tried to reason with him, indicating that no one could possibly love Mary more than Jesus himself loved her. Fr Konstanty at times became verbally abusive to Maximilian. Further doubts riddled young Konstanty, who even wrote to the Order's superiors in Poland and Rome, suggesting fancifully that Fr Kolbe wanted to found a new Order distinct from the Franciscans. After sowing seeds of discontent, Fr Konstanty eventually returned to Poland. He would later be killed during World War II. Meanwhile, Fr Maximilian remained serene.

When the Franciscans held their Chapter meeting in Poland in 1933, Fr Kolbe was a delegate. The future of the Japanese mission was debated. Some of the discontent just referenced filtered into the discussion. Maximilian prayed, and smiled, and let the positive fruits of the mission's first three years speak for themselves. Fr Kornel Czupryk, the highly-respected Provincial of Kraków who was just ending his term of office, took a bold step to express his esteem for Fr Kolbe and to assure the continuation of the mission of *Mugensai no Sono*. He informed the friars that he would not accept re-election as Provincial, and instead he volunteered to join the mission in Japan. This course of action would effectively silence Fr Maximilian's critics. Fr Kornel would become the new Guardian of the friary in Nagasaki, while Fr Maximilian remained the Editor of the *Seibo no Kishi* magazine and Director of the Crusade.

The superior-subject relationship between Fr Kornel and Fr Maximilian gave inspiration to everyone who witnessed it. They formed a perfect match. The humility of one confirmed the humility of the other. Kornel relied on the common sense and worldly wisdom of Maximilian. In 1936, as Fr Kornel prepared to depart on a fund-raising trip to the United States of America, Maximilian reproached him for wearing too shabby of a suit. Kornel was rather startled by the reproach from someone so reputed for the observance of religious poverty as Maximilian. The latter replied: *"Please, Fr Guardian, you are going to America, where everyone cares about external appearance. You must not look shabby in this way, or they will disregard you. Americans must see that we are not only beggars who beg; they must respect us.*" The same day, Maximilian went shopping with Kornel for a new black suit. Fr Kornel related the story to the friars at St Hyacinth Seminary in Granby, Massachusetts, when he visited there during that fundraising trip. Five decades later, at the age of ninety-five, Fr Kornel delighted to retell the story of St Maximilian and his shabby suit.

Return to the fatherland

Rumblings of war began to unsettle Europe in the mid-1930s. At the Polish Chapter of 1936, the need for Fr Maximilian's presence at *Niepokalanów* became urgently evident. The City of the Immaculate was now producing five different publications. The *Rycerz Niepokalanej* was approaching a circulation of nearly one million copies per month. *Niepokalanów* had its own seminaries, and even its own fire brigade. Its population had grown immensely. New vocations kept arriving every month. The uncertain clouds of possible war loomed over the future of the Crusade of Mary Immaculate and its global mission. Fr Maximilian's wisdom, holiness, and notable organizational skills would all be put to the supreme test. The Chapter elected him Guardian of *Niepokalanów*. Leaving his beloved Japan, he resolved to continue wearing his long beard, as a sign of solidarity with his brother missionaries in the Far East.

The friars who were left behind to carry on the Japanese mission would later give testimony about the future saint with whom they lived and worked. Brothers Zeno, Sergiusz, Romuald, Seweryn, Roman, Gregory, and Mieczysław were unanimous in describing their confrère Maximilian as a man of utmost confidence. His favourite scripture passage, frequently repeated to the friars, was a citation from St Paul's Letter to the Philippians: *"There is nothing I cannot master with the help of the One who gives me strength"* (*Ph* 4:13). Upon his return to *Niepokalanów* in 1936, these words of St Paul assumed even greater significance for Maximilian. He managed to incorporate them into his talks, homilies, and conferences with the friars and the laity. Often he would add to the sentence a closing tag *"through the Immaculata"*.

Poland again

In 1937, Fr Maximilian went to Rome and its environs for a fortnight to commemorate the twentieth anniversary of the founding of the Crusade of Mary Immaculate. He gave a number of conferences to Franciscan seminarians. Sensing a growing instability on the European continent, he used each talk to accent the theme of hope:

> "You are young, and therefore full of enthusiasm, but you must not let yourselves be discouraged... Rather than capitulate to scepticism, you should all the more be set afire for the apostolate...Jesus will not leave us alone, he is always living to intercede for us...and the Immaculate is always interceding for us...We must not trust in ourselves, but in the help of Jesus and of the Immaculate, to be fit instruments in their hands. We are comforted by the thought that good is more contagious than evil."(La Vigna, Rome, 31.I.37).

In private informal gatherings with the various seminarians of the Order in Rome, Fr Maximilian tried to reinforce the lads' vocations. Friar Patrick Griffin from Moycullen, Co. Galway, Ireland, later recalled meeting Fr Maximilian at the Collegio Serafico in the seminary stairwell. Several young friars surrounded the bearded Guardian of *Niepokalanów*. He managed to focus his eyes on each of the seminarians, and spoke to each in his own language: Italian, German, French, Polish. Since he did not speak Irish, he addressed Friar Patrick in Latin. He was preoccupied that each friar strive to conform his little will with the higher and larger Will of God - just as Mary Immaculate did. He stressed that God's Will is always good, and ultimately will triumph. In this conviction is our hope.

His major talk for the twentieth anniversary, delivered to cardinals, bishops, Roman nobility, university professors, and members of the major Franciscan families, in the Hall of the Immaculate at the Basilica of the Twelve Apostles, took place on the feast of Our Lady of Lourdes. He referred to her title "Immaculate Conception," and related it to the plan of God for the triumph of good over evil. Once more, he adduced reasons why believers must always claim grounds for hope, even when circumstances are threatening. To the assembled dignitaries, he made his famous and prophetic statement of hope that someday the white standard of the Immaculate would be raised high above the Kremlin in Moscow. (Ss. Apostoli, Rome, 11.II.37).

Another significant event occurred in the Crusade's twentieth anniversary year. Fr Maximilian enthusiastically embraced a new mode of evangelisation - radio. On the feast of the Immaculate Conception, he spoke on a *Radio Warsaw* broadcast to commemorate the tenth anniversary of the founding of *Niepokalanów*. Over the course of the next year, he worked to obtain the licence necessary for opening a radio station in *Niepokalanów*. Its first broadcast took place on the 11th of December 1938.

According to all of the testimonies, Fr Maximilian succeeded in bringing stability, growth, and hope to the community of friars at *Niepokalanów* in these years before World War II. Busy as he was, the Guardian always seemed to have time for each individual friar - no mean feat with over seven hundred and fifty residents. Fr Hyacinth Rosinke lived there through 1939, and later remembered his Guardian as a "simple, poor and sickly man, who had a very strong character, and set a vivid example for everyone on how to accept our crosses and conquer our difficulties with the help of God." He fostered fraternity among the men. Brother Felicissimus Sztyk never forgot the delight that his Guardian found in the simple pastime of watching the young friars play chess during their common recreation.

Setting a good example for the younger friars was always paramount for Maximilian. The sensitive humanity of the Guardian touched his friars in diverse ways. When Brother Roman Kwiecień was a postulant serving table, he noticed that Fr Maximilian had one of his legs crossed over the knee of the other leg. This was considered improper behaviour for a religious. Once noticed, other religious would have quickly put both feet on the floor. Not Maximilian; unflustered, he very naturally explained to Roman - so as not to scandalise him: *"Please do not judge. Understand my legs start to shake if I try to keep them together."*

Hospitality was another Franciscan virtue practiced by *Niepokalanów*'s Guardian. Numerous visiting friars passed through *Niepokalanów* during Fr Maximilian's final years there. Fr Conrad Miller remembers going for a bicycle ride with Maximilian, and eliciting the latter's compassion when Conrad's bike fell into a ditch. Fr Henry Senft remembered visiting *Niepokalanów* as a newly ordained young priest. Maximilian blessed and presented him with a handful of Miraculous Medals to take to America and distribute (two of those medals are in the possession of the author).

Fr Anthony Burakowski remembered visiting *Niepokalanów* with Fr Ferdinand Bakinowski, both of whom had previously met Fr Maximilian in Rome. The young friar-priests were invited into the refectory and seated at the top table beside the Guardian. The food was meagre, simply soup and barley. Concerned for his visitors, Maximilian turned to one of the brothers and said:

"These men are travelling and they need a little stronger food than what we have here; so you tell the cook to prepare a couple of pork chops. Let them eat something substantial so they will not faint on the way."

War

Two other visiting Franciscans from America, Fr Cornelian Dende and Fr Felix Mazur, found themselves in Warsaw on 1st September 1939. Both had been studying theology in Poland. Now they were both at the Franciscan curia in Poland's capital. Into the friary walked Fr Kolbe. He was carrying in hand a large piece of shrapnel - a fragment of bomb that had exploded that morning near the fence at *Niepokalanów*. It was the first day of the World War II. The Nazis had invaded Poland, and were bombing urban sites. Only one bomb fell on *Niepokalanów*, and there were no casualties. Fr Kolbe journeyed to Warsaw to confer with the Minister Provincial. They decided that the best plan of action would be temporarily to disband the friary, sending everyone to their families and home towns. Fr Maximilian returned to *Niepokalanów* to inform the friars of the decision. Thirty-six of the brothers, a Korean cleric, and one priest begged to remain with him at the City of the Immaculate. He agreed, entrusting all of them to the protection of their Immaculate patroness.

The next decision that he made was to get rid of his long beard, so as to be less conspicuous in days ahead when the Nazi invaders approached the friary. He reckoned that his

Franciscan habit would be provocation enough. Shaving the beard might buy him a few more days to work unnoticed. He summoned his barber, Brother Kamil, into his second-floor office. Once the barber completed the job, Fr Maximilian noticed that Kamil was wrapping the beard in a cloth, as if to preserve it. Maximilian insisted that the barber cast the wrapped beard into the stove which sat in the corner of his room. Obediently Brother Kamil complied.

Brother Kamil noticed, however, that there was no fire in the stove. Later, when Fr Maximilian had left the room, Kamil returned to remove the beard from the stove. This action would prove significant in subsequent years, at the time of the beatification and canonisation of St Maximilian. Because Fr Kolbe's body was cremated in the ovens of Auschwitz, the only first class relics of his mortal remains would be the hairs of his beard which Brother Kamil the barber had preserved. In the mid-1960s, the Minister General of the Order, Fr Basil Heiser, personally carried a large portion of the beard to Rome, still leaving a substantial portion behind for the archives of *Niepokalanów*.

On 19th September, the Nazis arrested Fr Kolbe and the remaining friars of *Niepokalanów*. They allowed two to remain in the infirmary. The friary was sacked, the presses sealed, and the statue of the Immaculate decapitated - the original statue that Fr Maximilian had placed in the fields of Prince Jan Drucki Lubecki fourteen years earlier. The friar-prisoners were transported to prison in boxcars. Between the time of their arrest until their eventual release on 8th December, they were incarcerated in three gaols: Lamsdorf, Amtitz, and Ostrzeszów. When they returned to *Niepokalanów* on 9th December 1939, Fr Kolbe straightaway inaugurated perpetual adoration of the Holy Eucharist - the still point of their turning world.

Within a week of Fr Kolbe's release from prison and return to the City of the Immaculate, refugees began thronging towards Warsaw along the Poznań road, which passed *Niepokalanów*. Altogether three and a half thousand displaced persons from the northwest of Poland would seek refuge at *Niepokalanów*. Among them there were fifteen hundred Jewish men, women, and children. Fr Maximilian welcomed the refugees into the friary, and determined to show them true Franciscan hospitality. He remembered the many Jewish businessmen who had been early benefactors of *Niepokalanów*, when it was first established in 1927. One generous Jewish crate merchant, while giving Brother Zeno an extra crate for free, had remarked, "*I'd like to have a nail at the monastery.*" Another Jewish merchant, giving an extra stool to Brother Zeno, similarly had remarked, "*I'd like to have a seat in the monastery.*" Now the friars could repay their Jewish brethren, not only with nails and seats, but food, beds, and fraternal charity.

On New Year's Day 1940, Fr Kolbe organised a special party at *Niepokalanów* for all of the Jewish children. He and the brothers presented them with sweets and other gifts. Fr Kolbe pleaded with the Nazi occupation authorities to allow the refugees to remain at *Niepokalanów*; however, the orders were given in February for their forcible eviction. One of the reasons for the Nazis' insistence on evicting the refugees was their desire to punish *Niepokalanów* for all of the defamatory articles and cartoons against Hitler and the Third Reich which had appeared in issues of the *Mały Dziennik*. The friars grieved helplessly as they bade the itinerant refugees goodbye. It is believed that not one of them survived the war. During the period when the refugees were accommodated in *Niepokalanów*, there were threats that Fr Maximilian might again be arrested. He could have left Teresin to seek sanctuary in a safer friary elsewhere in Poland or abroad. He steadfastly refused to desert his flock.

During the Nazi occupation, Fr Maximilian had one overriding goal - to resume publishing his monthly magazine, the *Rycerz Niepokalanej*. Persistently he approached the Nazi occupation authorities. Finally, they gave consent. A single wartime issue was published, dated December 1940/January 1941. In that issue, the feature article by Fr Kolbe was entitled "*Prawda*" ("Truth"). Its text was straightforward, and seemingly not inflammatory. Fr Kolbe asserted that there can be only one truth: it is all powerful; it is found in religion; and it is our lasting happiness. This article would prove to be the last published by Fr Maximilian in the *Rycerz*. Fittingly it serves as bookend to his first article in the *Rycerz* eighteen years earlier, where he asked the question *"Where is Happiness?"* The Nazis were greatly annoyed and dismayed by Fr Kolbe's audacity in raising the subject of truth. His doom was sealed.

One month after this single wartime issue of the *Rycerz* was published, Fr Kolbe was arrested again. On the morning of 17th February 1941, he woke early in his room at *Niepokalanów*. Perhaps he had a premonition. He summoned his secretary, Brother Arnold Wedrowski, to come straightaway to take dictation. With inspired urgency, Maximilian composed his final meditation on the mystery of the Immaculate Conception. Reverting to the question posed at Lourdes by Bernadette to Our Lady, Maximilian asked rhetorically: *"Who are you, O Immaculate Conception?"* He then concentrated on the relationship of Mary as the created Immaculate Conception to the Holy Spirit as the uncreated Immaculate Conception. With theological subtlety, he accented Mary's personhood as relational - standing unique between God and the human race. His act of total consecration to the Immaculata enabled him to participate in her unique relationship to God. That relationship can be summed in one word: love.

Auschwitz

With love foremost on his mind, he was ready for whatever God would ask of him. At 9:50 am the Gestapo arrived in two cars. They arrested Fr Kolbe and four other friar-priests. All five were taken from *Niepokalanów* dressed in their Franciscan habits, and driven to the notorious Pawiak Prison in the centre of Warsaw. A few days later, in a crowded cell holding Jewish and Catholic prisoners together, a sadistic SS officer became enraged at the sight of Fr Kolbe's Franciscan habit. He beat Maximilian across the face with the crucifix of the Franciscan rosary (the "crown" of Mary's seven joys) that hung from the three-knotted rope around the friar's waist. Repeatedly the SS man asked Maximilian: "*Priest, do you believe in this?*" Courageously affirming "Yes" each time, Fr Kolbe became victim to blow upon blow, falling bloodied to the floor. Meanwhile twenty brothers of *Niepokalanów* wrote to the Nazi Chief of Security offering to take the places of the five friar-priests. Their request was denied, as the Chief indicated that Fr Kolbe, leader of the community of friars, was the Nazis' principal enemy.

On 28th May, Fr Kolbe was transported in a cattle car with three hundred and four other prisoners from Pawiak to Auschwitz (in Polish, *Oświęcim*). Maximilian led his fellow prisoners in singing the famous Polish hymn to Our Lady *Serdeczna Matko* ("Beloved Mother"). The tones reverberated through the cattle car. Fr Maximilian Kolbe was already formulating his spiritual battle plan.

Upon arrival at Auschwitz, the prisoners entered through Auschwitz's main gate, with its mocking words *Arbeit Macht Frei* ("Work Sets You Free"). As he gazed at those words, Fr Kolbe would have remembered in counterpoint a different phrase about freedom, words from Scripture: *"The truth shall set you free"* (*Jn* 8:32). As the prisoner number tattooed on his arm would indicate, Fr Kolbe became the sixteen-thousandth-six-hundred-and-seventieth inmate to enter through those gates - #16670 - a passage of no return. Because Fr Kolbe's name was well-known throughout Poland owing to the wide circulation of his magazine, a buzz quickly spread among the prisoners. Francis Mleczko (#7481) remembered their astonishment, *"Fr Kolbe is here with us. The Nazis even got Fr Kolbe."*

As at every other phase of his life, Fr Maximilian, relying on God's grace, mediated through the maternal love of Mary Immaculate, assessed the situation and formulated his plan of action. Auschwitz for him would be a type of laboratory setting to prove that Gospel values were stronger than Nazi ideology. The captors aimed to create an atmosphere of fear, survival of the fittest, every man for himself, dog eat dog. The friar-priest Maximilian aimed to use the confinement as an occasion for faith-formation and mutual charity. Two diametrically-opposed world views would vie for supremacy in the two and a half months that Maximilian would live in Auschwitz. Franciszek Gajowniczek (#5659) testified that:

> *"Fr Kolbe organised prayer groups in our block in the evening when we returned from work. He would pray with the prisoners, encouraging them not to give up, to look forward to tomorrow, that the war would end, and we would be united with our families. These prayer groups were very helpful. They gave us hope."*

Some inmates in the same barracks as Maximilian would secretly creep to his bed at night, asking for counsel or for the sacrament of confession. One of them, Professor Joseph Stemler, later testified that the advice given him by Maximilian was simple and challenging: "*Hatred destroys; love alone creates.*" Above all, Fr Kolbe taught, we must not give into the temptation to hate those who are hurting us. If we hate them, then they have won. Love alone must triumph. Several of the prisoners like Ted Wojtkowski (#339) felt that the love motif was far more easily said than done. Speaking about Fr Kolbe's acts of charity towards his fellow prisoners, Ted reflected, "*I wouldn't have even been able to do this for my own mother - I was so scared.*"

Francis Mleczko strove to maintain a positive and upbeat spirit - solely because he knew that his survival depended upon his attitude. Even he, however, reached a point of despondency. It was then that Fr Kolbe took him aside to talk about the spirituality of total consecration to Mary, advising Francis to entrust his whole being to her loving motherly care. Forty years later, Francis Mleczko attributed that advice, and his putting it into practice, as the single most important factor that enabled him to survive Auschwitz. Mother Teresa of Calcutta reflected in a similar vein on Fr Kolbe's use of consecration to Mary as a remedy to fear and despair:

"When I think of St Maximilian Kolbe, I hear Jesus saying to me again, 'Love, to be true, to be real must cost, must hurt.' St Maximilian Kolbe knew what that meant, he knew how to love like Jesus. His life of giving until it hurt began long before he went to the concentration camp. That is why he could keep the joy of loving Jesus in his heart until the very end and share that joy with all with whom he came in contact. Who was his help in this? Who taught him the joy of giving until it hurt? Our Lady - to whom St Maximilian had entrusted everything. The same will be true of us. If we entrust ourselves to Our Lady, the Cause of Our Joy, she will teach us the joy of loving like Jesus." (Letter of Mother Teresa to Fr James McCurry, 20.I.95)

Mleczko, Wojtkowski, Gajowniczek, and several other contemporaries of Fr Kolbe in Auschwitz witnessed "bread" incidents - where Fr Kolbe, weak and emaciated, would break his bread ration in half to share it with a needy fellow prisoner. Tadeusz Pietrzykowski (#77) even witnessed a prisoner steal bread right out of Fr Kolbe's hands. When Tadeusz offered him another piece, Maximilian graciously took the bread from Tadeusz, walked over to the thief who had stolen from him, and gave the thief half of the new portion. Maximilian's love strategy displayed itself in varied ways.

None of the prisoners who had come to know Fr Kolbe during their shared incarceration would be surprised by the events which unfolded in late July 1941. It almost seemed that he had already planned his strategy for such an event. One of the prisoners escaped. In reprisal the camp overseer (Lagerführer) Fritsch forced all of the inmates of the escapee's barracks to stand for hours in the hot summer sun. Ten were to be selected for death by starvation in a subterranean bunker. This was the third time that Ted Wojtkowski stood in such a line-up. When Lagerführer Fritsch walked up and down the rows, he stopped at Francis Mleczko, told him to open his mouth, and looked for gold teeth. Francis was spared because he still had all of his own white teeth. Among the ten selected, however, was Franciszek Gajowniczek. A former sergeant in the Polish army, Mr Gajowniczek and his wife Helena had two teenage sons, Pawel and Juliusz. He exclaimed, *"What will become of my family? My poor family."*

Divine love in action

Moved by the plight of the father of a family, Fr Kolbe took immediate action. He stepped forward through the ranks of his fellow prisoners, and coming before the Lagerführer, he asked to be substituted for Gajowniczek. The Lagerführer addressed him scornfully as a "Polish swine," and asked who he was. Fr Kolbe's reply was an identity statement: *"I am a Catholic priest."* Remarkably, instead of simply adding an eleventh victim, the Lagerführer allowed Franciszek Gajowniczek to be spared. Wordless, Gajowniczek thanked Fr Kolbe with his eyes. Maximilian and the other nine were marched to the *Blok Śmierci* ("Block of Death"), then forced to undress, and locked naked in the underground death chamber. They would be given neither food nor water. Mockingly a wooden toilet sat in the corner.

Fr Maximilian's strategic plan of love without limits now reached its ultimate moment. Having ministered as a Catholic priest by freely offering to sacrifice his life for another, he would now in the death chamber minister to the other nine condemned. Evoking the image of Jesus Christ in chapter 25 of the Gospel of St Matthew, Fr Kolbe would now identify in the bunker with the hungry, thirsty, naked, homeless, sick and imprisoned men condemned to death. While they all still had strength, he led them in the singing of religious hymns to God and Mary. They prayed the Rosary aloud. Never before had the other prisoners outside heard prayers and songs emanating from the small window of the death cell. Previously only cries and shrieks punctuated the death agony of the condemned.

The prisoner-orderly Bruno Borgowiec (#1192) was tasked to remove the bodies of the dead from the bunker each day. After nearly a fortnight, there were still four left alive - barely. In the stillness of the morning of 14th August, the camp physician administered a lethal injection of drugs (carbolic acid) into each of the four. When Borgowiec entered to collect the corpses, he later testified, the body of Fr Kolbe, sitting propped against the wall, glowed with an ethereal luminosity. The bodies were carried to the crematorium. On the Solemn Feast of the Assumption, the "Martyr of Charity" was cremated.

About three kilometres from the camp, a marsh land in the hamlet of Harmęze was used as the dumping ground for most of the remains. The ashes were used there by the Nazis in various agricultural experiments. Those fields of Harmęze lay fallow for decades after the liberation of Auschwitz concentration camp in 1945. When Communism fell in 1989, the Franciscan Friars Conventual were able to obtain a small tract of land in Harmęze, and subsequently built a church at the site. The new church was erected as close as possible to the final resting place of the "Martyr of

Charity" and all of his fellow victims. When the friars were building the church, they made an astonishing discovery. For centuries, the little hamlet of Harmęze has had its own local coat of arms - a crest depicting a blank field with two crowns. Hence, St Maximilian Kolbe's lifelong journey of the two crowns literally ended at the place of the two crowns, where, by the love of God, he exchanged the white and the red for one of gold.